INVITATION TO INSIGHT

Invitation to Insight

Meditative Poems
by Stephanie Noble

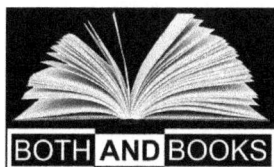

BOTH **AND** BOOKS

Invitation to Insight
Meditative Poems by Stephanie Noble

Copyright 2023 Stephanie Noble.

All Rights Reserved
Both/And Books

ISBN 978-0-9638088-9-9

stephanienoble.com

Cover photo: Will Noble
Book design: Adrian Emery

More books by Stephanie Noble

*Asking In: Six Empowering Questions
Only You Can Answer*

*Tapping the Wisdom Within,
A Guide to Joyous Living*

Dedicated with deep bows
to the teachers. staff & volunteers
of Spirit Rock Meditation Center
and to all my students,
my Sangha Sisters, over the years.

In memory of beloved teachers
Janice Gates and Wes Nisker

Introduction

Poetry isn't meant to explain the wisdom teachings. Instead, poetry can slip us into the side door of the meditation hall and assure us we belong. It whispers on a breeze from the woods outside the hall, reminding us why we've come.

When a teacher ends a silent sitting by reading a poem, it can resonate like the bell bowl's sustained ring. Having quieted our minds and cultivated a more spacious heart, the poem rings true. Then it stays with us, shifting and deepening our understanding.

I've written and given many dharma talks over the years, and they contain imagery and metaphors to help my readers and listeners understand and remember the concepts shared. But out of my own daily practice and many silent retreats, the natural expression that arises is poetry.

The poems in this volume are that expression. May they open the heart to understanding. May they be an invitation to insight.

- SN 2023

Contents

Fleeting Beauty

Why do I pause
to view a rainbow in awe?

What is a rainbow?
A fleeting comingling of four elements:
fire, earth, water, and air
in the form of
sunlight, dust, raindrops, and sky

What am I?
A fleeting comingling of four elements:
fire, earth, water, and air
in the form of
energy, bone, blood, and breath

So why don't I pause
in awe of this
and this
and this
of every fleeting moment of being?

The Perch

Dense ground fog of January's cold,
bare black oak a deeper gray, where
birds blend in like lingering leaves
then lift off to melt into mist.

The highest limb has a gnarly top
a jutting branch a right angle lop,
an amateur hacked some years back,
a fault revealed only in winter.

That awkward knob is an ideal perch
for birds of prey, just the way
a once-botched dream turns out to be
the very one that suits us.

Let them all come in

Let them all come in.
Open the door gently
so they won't fall on their faces
but let them all come in.
Careful now, don't crush the hand
that seeps under the doorsill.
Don't stab too hard
the key into the hole
through which an eye's
been watching,
waiting.
Yes, let them all come in.
I'm just too tired to listen
to their scratching
and their whining.
I want to see their faces

and be done with them.

Isolated Incident?

Could this possibly be

an isolated incident?

seed

    shoot

        leaf

            bud

                blossom

                    petals

                fall to the ground.

Could I possibly be

the exception to the rule?

spring

    summer

        fall

            winter

spring again

All around me, the world is spinning in cycles

Could my life be the lone straight line?

Oak Sisters

Three oaks entwine on the hillside:
Minoan snake goddesses with burled breasts.

I, with the good fortune to sit below them,
rarely bow in gratitude,

while they bow to the wind, the rain,
the sun and the moon.

I am footloose, but rarely dance,
while they, despite earthly constraints,

sway together in ecstasy.
I imagine underground a mirror dance

of roots rollicking round rock,
deeper and deeper into the soil of being.

Whatnot

It's not mine to name or claim,
not yours nor his, it's all the same.

The densely crammed attic of a packrat fanatic,
filled to the gills till the floorboards groan
with knickknack curios, baubles, and bibelots,

all on loan from a honeycombed catacomb
where nothing's measured ounce for ounce
and there are no words to mispronounce,

Yet sounds abound like a babbling stream
and every dream of every sleeper, every thought
and even deeper in the heap are
untold riches and unscratched itches,
ravines of gold and offal ditches.

All of a piece absorbed unjudged,
sweet and sour, sludge and fudge.

A repository of every story
ever told within the fold
of creatures bold and critters shy,
how they lived and how they died,
how they felt, how hard they tried,
how they laughed and how they cried.

Every season everywhere,
every joy, every despair,
every curse and every prayer.

And underneath each fallen leaf,
each lost belief, each sigh of relief,
each hollow heart trapped in its grief,
are earthy odors rich and moist
of every word that's left unvoiced.

When the day

When the day
gets away from me

I give it a getaway car
and let it drive
its restless ramble.

On a round earth
held by gravity
what's the harm
in letting go?

Creek Bed Meditation

Friday mornings at Spirit Rock, I walk the land.
I have chaperoned butterflies dancing,
sat with water skates playing in ponds,
listened to the earth's symphony of birds, frogs, crickets
and water trickling in the creek.

Each week I note the subtle shifting of the seasons
as they seed, grow, ripen, and fade before my eyes.
Winter-dampened fog-shrouded hills,
tree bark and boulders gilded with emerald moss,
bounding water gushing forth -- all give way:
wet to dry, green to yellow, cold to hot.

Now in mid-summer, the morning air is dry and still,
the hills are golden, the frogs are quiet.
I enter the dappled shelter of a laurel grove,
and descend into the rocky creek bed.
Its deep banks rise around me,
swallowing me whole.
Night chill held in the rocks
along with the vague memory of water
rises to cool my skin.
Beneath my feet leaves crunch and crackle
in the hush of morning.
The shaggy yellowed tree moss
hangs loose and dusty.
Gnarled roots dangle over the dry creek, searching.
I duck under fallen logs
following the cavernous twists and turns
of the underpinnings that shape

winter's waterfalls and spring's deep pools.
Not even a puddle remains.

It seems I am the only water here.
The air tingles with a dowsing awareness
of my wet presence in the midst of dry longing.

I feel the flow of myself as I move downstream.

Now is a demanding mistress

Now is a demanding mistress.
She'll take you in the checkout line,
transform tedium into festivity
as tender as a wedding.

Now is a demanding mistress.
Ignore her at your peril!
It's more than mismatched socks,
faux pas and fender benders.

One mindless sideways glance
and boom: The morgue.
Or the pain of searing remorse.
Well, she warned you not to look away.

Yes, Now is a most demanding mistress,
but she gives you that orgasmic glow.
With her, it's all or nothing, baby.
Are you in?

Chaos Theory

In the very earliest times
when crocodiles had lion dreams
and crows nested in the imaginations of buffalo,
everything was fluid, burgeoning, and vibrant.
The colors were so changeable
chameleons could not keep up.

Then someone woke up one morning exhausted,
cranky from his wild bee dreams, and said, 'Enough!'
He began to draw lines, build fences,
and establish a proper hierarchy.

But no one noticed.

So, he designed a creator in his image,
and told him to *please, stop this chaos!*
Can we just have a little order here?
And the Creator,
flush with the rush of newly vested power,
called out to his rank and file,
You hippopotami, go over to that river
on that continent and get a grip.
Stop messing about with the tigers' heads.

Oh sure, there was some grumbling,
but everyone heeded the edict
because a bit of calm sounded pleasant
before resuming the wild fiesta of life.

Haven't you ever had a moment
when you just wanted things to settle?
To see all the books and toys
lined up neatly on the shelf?

But even as you arranged them
in tidy rows by topic or color,
you never in a million years
thought they should stay

on the shelves forever
without being played with,
without being read,

as if that's where they belong
instead of in the hands
of those with imagination
and a willingness to play.

The Running Child Meditation

In the foyer of the meditation hall
a small child runs back & forth
back and forth, feet plopping & rising
& pausing & turning again.

Inside the sitting room a meditator
feels irritation rising within her.
"What could that parent be thinking?
Why don't they take that child outside?"

Another meditator is drawn
into a memory of her own children, now grown,
and the sweetness of the footfalls in the foyer.

Another notes in awe the boundless energy
of youth and feels her own lethargy.
"I am old," she sighs.

Yet another is caught in the aching emptiness
of the old dream of the child she never had.
She hadn't expected it to find her here
and feels a victim of its intrusion.

Another doesn't notice the sound very much,
so loud are her own thoughts, planning, planning.

Another doesn't hear the sound at all.
She is almost asleep in a fog and nodding,
catching her head each time it drops.

Another hears the sound as simple sound,
unattached to any image –
a rhythmic cadence, soft and round.

Another composes a poem in her head, titled
The Running Child Meditation.

And all of these are me.

Dirt Bag Dharma

I don't know how long I had been ill.
Long enough to see myself as
fragile, wan, weak, in need of protection
from violent images and emotion
that could suck the life right out of me.

But I needed soil for my garden
and the young worker assigned to shovel
ten bags of dirt for me was apparently
way overdue for a break, and no doubt
had other grievances fueling his anger.

I backed off -- to give him space, I thought,
but really more to give *me* space,
as I retreated to the cocoon of my car to wait.

Feeling guilty, I began to send him Metta:
May you be well. May you feel at ease.
At first, the words had a begging quality
like the prayers of a small child, cowering
in a corner, terrified of the boogeyman.

But the words became an invocation
And suddenly I saw myself more clearly:
how knotted in fear I seemed,
as knotted as the worker out there
both of us suffering our grievances.

The blessing became a shaft of light
breathing into me, releasing me

from my victim stance, revealing instead
my capacity to be a conduit
of compassionate healing energy.

Across the muddy yard, I saw him too.
still shoveling dirt into bags,
still bent, still angry, still suffering.
So, I returned to his side and soon
we were chatting -- who knows about what,
it didn't matter, because -- all the while
I breathed in his suffering and out that radiant light.

Soon his shoulders softened,
and his voice lost its edge. I heard a low
chuckle at something I said,
and when his boss yelled another order,
he didn't bark or bristle as he'd done before.
Instead, he smiled at me, and rolled his eyes as if to say,
'Maybe it's not much, but it's mine and I can handle it.'

At that moment, standing in the mud,
amidst my ten bags full of dirt,
it dawned on me
that I am well.

Storm at Last

What could be better than
to watch the deep clouds gather in the West,
to thrill at the first blast of wind rattling the house,
to welcome the first splatter of drops upon the deck.
to delight in how branches frolic and bow,
to listen to the patter on the skylight.

Grateful not to be caught out in the storm,
blown along by blinding pelts of cold rain.
Safe inside, snug and warm, teacup in hand,
mesmerized by the circle dance on the slickened deck
and the way drops race down the window glass.

To all driving blindly in this storm
To all huddled under freeway overpasses
To all who hunger in the cold and wet:

May you be well.
May you be safe.
May you somehow
find joy, even now.

Shedding

A snake sheds its skin slowly.
There must be days when the skin
is a drag on movement,
when the desire to rub up
against some rough bark
is overwhelming.

Or is that just me, projecting
my own longing to be shed
of all the dead, dried
and dragging within me?

I envision the snake one day
noticing a fresh sleekness and fluidity
and slithering sensuously
through the tall grass.

A deciduous tree too has no choice
about when its leaves finally
accept the wind's invitation
to be borne aloft and tumble down.

Does it feel loss, that tree,
stripped of its veil of foliage?
No, that's just me again,
caught up in my own fears
of barren winter, not
considering all that unseen
rooting and renewing.

Somehow it soothes me to see
that the snake is not its skin
nor the tree its leaves.
Even though it must have seemed so
until that very moment of release.

Crossing the Stream

Crossing the stream, arms akimbo,
I teeter on one steppingstone while testing
for solidity of the next before giving over,
yet again, total reliance on a rock that may wobble.

With information, too, sometimes I lose balance,
stumbling upon Wikipedia discussions
hurling opposing rocky facts. I duck
and dodge getting hit in the crossfire --
like which side of the Nepal-India border
is Lumbini, the birthplace of the Buddha?

Now I shed my shoes to walk the riverbed.
No need to test, tentative, or teeter, tensed.
Instead, I sense the river pulsing on my ankles
as I wade in the cool, clear rapids.

Then I slowly let myself go and sink up to my shoulders
in a quiet pool in the shade of an alder tree.
Dark buoyancy holds me lightly.
The point of my chin softens in wavering circles
spreading out from the dappled dance of water skates.

Yes, rocks may give water a course to run,
and the interplay of the two is a glory to behold.
But truth be told, water runs, rocks or no,
along the path of least resistance,
flooding fields and lapping shores.

Just so the dharma dances beyond ideas of borders,
sweet and bracing as clear water
beneath verdant boughs on a sweltering summer day.

Wanderlust

Hey, wanderer!
Pack me in your rucksack
so I can see the view
without having to
read a map,
chart the course,
make reservations
or plan anything at all.

Instead, I'll nestle here
all snug amidst your
apple, cheese, and bread
poking my head out
to sniff the lavender fields
of Provence and see
the Pyrenees without
my knees
begrudging the journey.

Bondage

"What holds you in bondage?"
The dharma question insinuates itself
into my thoughts for weeks.
I hadn't thought I was in bondage
but the question refuses to rest.

Aha!

Suddenly I can see: It is my habitual nature
that holds me in bondage.
My habitual nature trudges
in ever-deepening and narrowing ruts.
My treasured patterns weave a thick web
that cocoons me from really seeing.
Shaken awake, I celebrate.

"But *why* does my habitual nature
hold me in bondage?"
Yet another dharma dilemma arises unbidden
to dog me for yet more weeks.

Aha!

My predictable patterns
create a sense of permanence.
My habitual nature is trying
to construct a safe world
that will be there in the morning.

But permanence is a delusion!

Nothing is permanent.
My habitual nature may want to
protect me, but it only shields me
from the fresh light of awareness.

Ah.

May I see anew in every moment.

May all beings see anew in every moment.

Ode to Japanese Maple in a Courtyard

My hand upon your trunk, a kindred hum,
Earthy greetings rise from your roots
Sunny salutations as your leaves
flutter brushing cheek and inner arm
My roaming hands stroke your limbs
The rough-on-rough of kindred skin
I rub the rounds of your old wounds
and feel guilt for all my pruning
curse my need to impose my sense
of order on those whose nature
is to grow in symbiotic celebration
of earth and light and rain
Get lost in excuses: This is not my tree
These wounds are not my doing
You interrupt me quizzically:
Who is this 'my' this 'you' this 'tree?'
Words throw up fences, cages
make no sense, can't engage us
I reach my arm along a limb
My side aligns to sink within
I breathe out, you breathe in
You breathe out, I breathe in
Know only this: we are kin.

Shadow

Shadow lies like a rug,
or at least stretches
the truth with the
downing sun.

Shadow hugs
the ground
and prays
at the altar
of whatever
passing god
shields it
from the
light.

Doubt

Doubt
is the tidal crush of my castle
before I feel the sand beneath me

Doubt
is my reflection in a puddle
before I lift my head to the sky

Doubt
is the drained light after sunset
before I hear the gulls' cry

Doubt
is undertow knocking me flat
before I feel the lift of the sea

Nameless

Who calls my name?

> *No one!*

Does Oneness call out to itself?

Seeking recognition I separate,
and then despair at the loneliness
of my unseen state.

But it is only separation that is unseen.
Oneness sees, knows, and loves me.

There is no need for naming.

Dragon at the Gate

In the West
we've had dragons
knights reached
sainthood
by slaying.

In the East
the dragon
waits at the gate
of nirvana.

Sit with your dragon
until it wags its tail,
licks your hand and
lets you pass.

Earthlings All

We all descend from original people,
traditional people with tribal ways.

Not one of us is a stranger here,
regardless of where or how
the winds of change
transplanted us
or our ancestors.

Those ancestors whisper opinions
in our ears, full of fear
of what appears for them,
new and different.

We catch their familiar homey scent
and may feel called
to recreate their world
back to the way we think it was,

but this
-- Look around! --
is our world now.
None of us is alien.
We are earthlings, all.

The Wanderer

In your country I find the angle of light
has shifted, wobbling my gait.

You pass by, avert your eyes,
thus miss:

> How the rock swallows the sun
> then shares it with the lizard.

> How the quiver of bamboo performs
> a shadow dance on the terrazzo walls.

> How orange koi gather in the depths
> of the pond, sheltered in the shade.

Sad how, for fear of me,
you lose the wanderer in you.

The Trouble with Home

The trouble with home is how it calls to you --
a seashell whisper on some distant strand.
Foam enlaces your ankles, then
sucks hollows beneath your feet.

The trouble with home is how it supports you --
rocks studded in the stream. You teeter.
from stone to stone, tensed against
slippery descent into the flow.

The trouble with home is how it cradles you --
a nest in the crook of a craggy oak. You gaze
across acres of wind-bowed grasses
and feel the phantom ache for wings.

Clinging

Sometimes life feels like
sitting in an over-air-conditioned theater
on a sweltering summer day,
having forgotten to bring a sweater,
watching a horror movie
that raises my hair on end
and my shoulders, neck, and jaw
are whipped to a frigid froth
of tension more caffeinated
than a frozen frappe.

Yet I stay seated
caught up in the plot
and dreading
the heat outside.

Even though the warmth
would soften the tight chill
and the trees would give
a sweet, dappled light
as I lie on the grass,
melting into the earth,
listening to the birds,
the creek, and the voices
of people as they stroll by,

feeling at ease at last
in the lyrical lull
of simply being

alive.

Patent Pending

This freewheeling synaptic relay
bathed in adrenaline and hormones
I confess is not my personal invention.

Yet as it processes sensory impressions
categorizing in descending order from
delicious pleasure to horrendous pain,
and then shuffles, examines and
evaluates past content for future reference,

I forget. I think I have a patent pending
and ponder product branding,
design my logo and packaging,
form focus groups from familiar faces
to develop a new improved version

of something it turns out is
a generic inherently unpatentable
not to mention unpackageable
universal process. Useful, but not
alas, unique, and not, alas, mine.

Phew!

Elemental

I understand water
following the path
of least resistance.

I understand fire
the burning need
to consume.

I understand earth
the dense compacted
gravity of being.

But air?
With each breath, I wonder
how my life can depend
on something that seems
barely there.

Flight

Perched on a tottering tower of luggage,
counting on my fingers nibbled to nub,
sure that something's been left undone
in the early morning fog without coffee.

The airport shuttle pulls up the drive.
Both sliding doors spring open.
The driver hops out and tosses
suitcases in one door, but they fly

straight out the other. I watch
as they bounce down the hillside, clasps
bursting open – a flurry of unfurled
T-shirts, jeans, black dress pants, shoes,

repackaged cream, shampoo, and gel,
soaring laptop, camera, cell phone
all land askew in the gully, dingy
undies dangling from low branches.

I'm aghast at the litter but too stunned
for outrage. It seems a done deal.
He slams the doors shut and yells, 'Let's go!'

I hear 'Let go!' and pour into the van
light as chiffon on the breeze.
We lock eyes and start laughing
as he releases the brake.

Prodigal Mind

When my mind
returns to the breath
there is such a sense
of homecoming
such a celebration of
this most perfect union

that I would not be surprised
if the invitations were sent out
the band hired
and the cake decorated

were there only enough time
before my wayward mind
sets off to wandering again.

The To Do List

Like a junkie
with a rolled-up dollar bill,
the night sucks
the ink off the page
of the to-do list on the desk.

Ink enters my bloodstream,
then Rorscharchs into my dreams
and coagulates at the base
of my medulla oblongata.

I wake, sputtering.

Dead middle of the dank night,
probed by a fluorescent moon,

the universe, a giant generator
in the basement of a hulking building

where I, the janitor, lie sleepless
on a sagging cot in an adjacent closet,
responsible for EVERYTHING.

Night's a tight squeeze.
No breath all matter.
Colossal consequence compressed,
bullet point bowling balls crush toes.

I wail into the trail of the plummet.
Edges crumble. I stumble, sucked

into the black hole. Grateful.

Daylight reconstitutes space.

The recalcitrant to-do list
sits meekly on the desk, its
words crocheted into doily reminders
 – polite suggestions, really –
of how, were I so inclined,
I might spend my day

Every little letting go

Every little letting go
even a quarter inch or so
every surrender renders
such release

The still pond within
-- deep, dank, dark
and desperate
to be known

is no longer hidden
from the sunlight
of my willingness
to warm, to rise

in a mist of utter ease
to float in clouds
diffusing as they drift
away, away, away

The Dowser

The dowser with his wiggling sticks
locates the spot to sink the well,
so that deep into the earth
buckets drop and rise
full of sweet pure water.

I too am a dowser of sorts
locating the just right spot:
right here
right now
to sink a well of relaxation
where my breath drops and rises
pulling up the sweet pure infinite
coursing boundlessly within.

I have tried drilling other places,
other times, drifted lost in abandoned sites,
hauled my heavy gear thirstily toward a mirage.
The dowser would have told me
the ground is shallow everywhere but
right here
right now
and those buckets would come up empty.

Some doubt the dowser whose skill
can't be explained. He simply knows
how water sings
and lets go enough to listen.

May I too let go enough to listen
to what is
right here
right now.
May my sticks wiggle joyously
and my well sink effortlessly.
May these buckets quench the thirst
of all beings everywhere.

Butterfly in Benin

You know that butterfly in Benin
that by a flap of its fragile wings
sets into motion air currents
that gain strength across the Atlantic
to arrive as a hurricane
in the Caribbean?

When I catch myself caught up in
the currents of causes and conditions
I refocus and remember
these thoughts are only filaments
floating in perpetual patterns
whirling through me in passing
like the winds of the world.

The Gift

May I open
the gift of this moment
without expectation
anticipation
frustration

May I gently attend
its unwrapping

unentangled by
ribbon nooses
of my own making

undistracted
by tissue paper
patterns of
longing and despair

May the gift of life
amaze me
at every turn

May I greet
whatever is revealed
with gratitude
and wonder

Taming Anger?

I have not fed you
though you still skulk
in the cage I made you
to contain your beastly rage.

I have not fed you
though you linger
like some grumpy uncle
smelling sour from foul habits
but after all, still family.

I have not fed you
because if I did
you would push your way
to the front of the litter,
gobbling up everything,
leaving nothing for
the rest of me.

I have not fed you.
Instead, I cower
in corners, afraid
to let you into my heart
lest you devour all
that is good within me.

So, no!
I have not fed you.

But lately, I wonder
if I'm strong enough
to tame you, to feed you
compassion
so your power
is no longer ruthless
but valiant,
a noble champion.

So, I ask you now:
Can you prove yourself worthy?
Can your unwieldy power
burn steady and bright,
shining the way
like a lighthouse?

Or will you claw me
when I extend my hand
and open my heart.
Will I suffer regret
when you
sucker-punch me again?

Hard to know.

So here I wait,
well taught not to tangle,
not to tease, not to tempt,
not to test, not to trust you.

I stare through the bars
of your cage where you pace,
each forced turn in that tight space
an affront to your nature.

And I wonder.

The Weight of Certainty

Certainty
drapes across the chest
like a lead vest
in a dentist's chair.
A waking death
no eternal rest.
Just a pretense
of protection.

But protection from what?

From the breath
that is life.

From the love
that radiates
illuminating
all that is.

From the
possibility of
awe and wonder.

Jay Squawking

The scrub jay defends her territory,
seeing boundaries where I see none.
I begin to wonder about my boundaries:
How many of the barriers I see,
the assumptions I make about
limits and possibilities
can be seen by the jay?

Know-it-all

Make room for the know-it-all
though his manner be overbearing
without an ounce of doubt

or curiosity. He has only answers
contained and categorized,
knowledge a commodity neatly
stacked in his storeroom.

Make room as he passes!
His lumbering gait, under the weight
of such unwieldy treasure
knocks down all in his path.

Make room in your heart
to see his fear of not knowing,
of letting go, of losing
his grip on the trowel for

the mortar to shore
up the walls of his fortress
where he feels safe
to look down on those

dancing in light
vibrant with wonder.
At each turn, elation

echoing the revelation
I don't know!
    I don't know!
        I don't know!

        Hooray!

The Pause

The finch was stunned by its unexpected slam
into the glass door, reflecting the branches
it had meant to fly through.

It sat on the doormat quite still
but upright, not dead, or at least not yet.

From inside, I could see its eye blinking.
I never considered whether a songbird's eyes blink.

Minutes later, though nothing had visibly changed,
it flapped its wings and flew.
It went for the glass door once again
but so lightly it ricocheted, then away.

It had just needed to pause to recover.
As I do when I come up against something hard.

Distance

Here & now
things are
actual size
ready to be
dealt with.

Then & there
even big things
appear small.

This is not just
some artist's
trick of perspective.

Things in the distance
are small because there is
absolutely nothing
we can do about them
from here

except wrap them
in loving kindness
and return to
the breath.

Answers Everywhere

It is not the answers that are lacking.
They are everywhere:
In every leaf drifting to the ground,
in each bud bursting forth from seeming nothingness...

And the ocean! Now there's an answer for you!

Yes, the answers are everywhere,
eager to share sparkling tales
of beauty and energy abounding
in this fleeting, precious gift of life.

But we, in our heavy-headed habit,
burrow further into our cocoon.

So exhausted
from the struggle
of resisting the harsh blast,
of being sucked down
into the churning tangle
of so many painful thoughts

that innate curiosity dries up
and drifts off, leaving only
achy questions like, why me?

Could we but soften our gaze
relax the fist, ever ready for a fight

Allow the gentle mist of awareness
to refresh us, to renew our view.
Oh, why is it so hard to remember?
that one cherished breath
allows us to come home
allows us to wonder
with open-hearted curiosity
and even the gift of awe.

The Sacred Art of Eavesdropping

In the next chair at the hair salon
a client laments she's never been
to the Grand Canyon.

Her stylist, between clips, replies
'Well, it's nice and all, but really,
when you think about it, it's
just a big hole in the ground.'

I stare in the mirror and try
to imagine the hole in my life
had I never stood on the edge
overlooking the descending strata
of craggy ridges, nestled in shadow.

Awestruck by the shifting hues
of yellow ochre, orange, crimson and magenta,
as they waltz, polka and tango with light and moisture,
never the same view twice
even if I stood there forever.

I imagine the hole in my life
had I never stood on the edge
awestruck by the power of a river
to carve rock over eons of time
beyond my capacity to fathom,
humbled by the sudden
intimate awareness
of my infinitesimal existence,
cradled in the juxtaposition
of a fleeting yet infinite moment.

Just a few minutes before,
in conversation with *my* stylist,
I whined about the hassles
of a recent trip, and how I may be
getting too old to travel.

But now I wonder if the places
I let slide off my bucket list
are not mere boxes unchecked

but holes in my soul beckoning me to be holy.

In Celebration of the Winter Solstice

Why be afraid of the darkness?
Dark is the rich fertile earth
that cradles the seed, nourishing growth.

Dark is the soft night that cradles us to rest.

Only in darkness
can stars shine across the vastness of space.

Only in darkness
is the moon's dance so clear.

There is mystery woven in the dark, quiet hours,
There is magic in the darkness.

Do not be afraid.
We are born of this magic.

It fills our dreams
that root, unravel and reweave themselves
in the shelter of the deep, dark night.

The dark has its own hue,
its own resonance, its own breath.

It fills our soul,
not with despair, but with promise.

Dark is the gestation of our deep and knowing self.

Dark is the cave where we rest and renew our soul.

We are born of the darkness,
and each night we return
to the deep moist womb of our beginnings.

Do not be afraid of the darkness,
for in the depth of that very darkness
comes a first glimpse of our own light,
the pure inner light of love and knowing.

As it glows and grows, the darkness recedes.

As we shed our light, we shed our fear
and revel in the wonder of all that is revealed.

So, do not rush the coming of the sun.
Do not crave the lengthening of the day.

Celebrate the darkness.
Here and now.

A time of richness.

A time of joy.

No Thread Left Unwoven

On retreat at Spirit Rock

Dried hills weave yellow ribbons
in the last light

They whisper
> *Leave no part of your being*
> *unwoven in the fabric of your life*

While the tidy seamstress with her
pursed lips full of straight pins
cuts frayed threads to the quick

The hills tell me
> *Even a weakness can be a strength*

How that hunger for approval
inspires me to offer praise

The hills say
> *Even a strength can be a weakness*

How that hunger for perfection
cuts away what is fine

Can I shed my shears?
Just let these threadbare tatters
weft at will through this life of mine?

The hills sing
> *Let it be so.*

Metta at Midnight

Awake again
mulling over painful events and poor decisions,

I know that, relatively speaking,
of course, I am lucky to have such paltry
problems in a week when tornados, cyclones
and earthquakes have killed tens of thousands
and left five million homeless.

I don't want to need the misery of others
to make my life seem good.
Still, the switch with which I beat myself
temporarily loses its sting.

Still awake, I begin to send blessings
over the mountains and across the plains
to flattened towns, where suddenly
small found objects mean so much
and so little.
>   *May you be well, may you be at ease.*

I send blessings across the Pacific
to families waiting and watching
piles of shattered concrete slabs and
twisted rebar for signs of life:
>   *May the ache in a Sichuan mother's chest be eased.*

Under the rubble, a small pool of rainwater
keeps a child alive until rescue comes.

> *May arms open to receive those*
> *wandering aimlessly, whose homes*
> *and worldly goods have crumpled into nothing.*
> *May the seeds of happiness already be planted*
> *amidst the wrenching pain.*

Blessings know no boundaries,
so, I am not surprised to find that
I am now sending them to those
who live in war-torn communities,
where fear is a constant companion:

> *May you find ease, may your heart know peace.*

And to those who see violence as a necessary evil:

> *May your hearts be softened,*
> *May you sense your connection.*

And blessings fly to lands stricken by drought
to those who sleep to forget their hunger,
and to all people everywhere who are
suffering pain in their body or mind,

to those who have recently lost the one they love best,
and those who have never had a love to lose,

and those who are sleeping in cars, under bridges,
in shelters, and those who have been abused,
and those who have lost themselves

and…oh my god, it just goes on and on, doesn't it?

But as I breathe in the pain of the world
and breathe out loving-kindness,
the hardened armor I carefully crafted to keep
the endless misery of the world at bay,
becomes porous, allowing the blessings to pour
through all the holes in a tidal exchange
until there is nothing but blessing.

So, I send blessings to the leaders.
> *May you sense your connection to all of life*
> *and respond with wisdom.*

I send blessings to the ravaged earth.
> *May you heal. And to its inhabitants:*
> *May you live in peace and know joy.*

I bring my blessings home to my neighborhood.
On this hot night, with windows and doors open,
I feel how all of us are resting together:
the birds, lizards, deer, squirrels, raccoons,
insects, and the humans behind screens,
snoring or lying wakefully worrying, or
feeling a pain magnified by night.
> *May we all find ease and take comfort in knowing*
> *that there is someone, maybe many people,*
> *who, even though we are unknown to them,*
> *are sending us loving kindness even now.*

The threads of infinite blessings weave
a dense brilliant web, a hammock of light.

And at last, I rest.

Yes!

The world is teeming with answers
to questions we don't bother to ask.

And most of the answers are *Yes!*

Whole mountains, lakes, and valleys.
Vast oceans, forests, deserts, and plains.

Brimming with life loving itself into being,
they all shimmer *Yes!* in the sunlight.
They all whisper *Yes* in the moonlight.

Yet some people only hear
the hissing sound
on the tail of all those esses:
YeSSSSSSSSSSSSSSSSS…

Frozen in fear,
they are too terrified
to go about in the world at all.

At home alone, afraid, they moan.
And their cries echo *Ooooooooh…*

So, if we are not careful listeners,
we might hear *Nooooooooooooo,*
and, thinking the world is against us,
we lock our doors up tight,

Forgetting to ask, *Is this true?*

So, ask your questions.
And make space for the answers.

Listen to the mountains, valleys, and oceans.
Listen to the forests, deserts, lakes, and plains.

All shimmering *Yes!* in the sunlight,
whispering *Yes* in the moonlight.

Yes! to your passionate wonder.

Yes! to your being you, just as you are:
life's precious gift to itself.

Index

About the Poet

Stephanie Noble has taught Buddhist Insight meditation since 2007 at Marin Insight Women's Sangha and guest-teaches at other sanghas. She serves on the board of the Buddhist Insight Network, an international non-profit that is the hub for insight teachers and sangha leaders.

Along with her personal meditation practice, she has attended, studied, volunteered, taught, and sat many retreats at Spirit Rock Meditation Center since 1994.

She has been twice nominated for the Pushcart Prize and her poems have been published in many anthologies and journals, including *The Buddhist Poetry Review*, *Light of Consciousness Magazine*; *The MindfulWord*, and *Unsilenced-the Spirit of Women*.

Stephanie has studied poetry writing extensively with Prartho Sereno, Marin County poet laureate emerita, and with Judyth Hill, Kim Stafford, and Anne Cushman. In 1980 she was one of a select group of poets chosen for a UC Berkeley extension course titled 'Poems in Progress: A Workshop with Six American Poets' taught by Alan Soldofsky, with guest teachers Margaret Atwood, Robert Bly, Gary Snyder, Caroline Kizer, and Philip Levine.

She lives in San Rafael, California with her husband, the artist Will Noble. They have been blessed with four children and five grandchildren.

For more information and many dharma posts, visit *stephanienoble.com*.

Acknowledgments

First and foremost, I thank my beloved husband Will Noble, who read all my poems aloud to me to save my challenged eyes.

Other help and encouragement came from friends Carol Griffin, Jane Wicklund, Sandy Neumann, and Ellen Mundell.

Thanks also to Prartho Sereno. This book would not have come into being had she not created Leapers, a small group of her Poetic Pilgrims she felt were ready to take the leap into book publication. And thanks to those Leapers who continue to inform, inspire, and celebrate each other. It really does take a village! And thanks to Linda Enders, author of *Consider the Gravity*, for generously hosting our gatherings.

For his always skillful help in bringing this book to life, I thank Adrian Emery.

My gratitude knows no bounds for Marleen Roggow, my friend and retired poetry agent, who, over several years, sent out my poems to publications so I wouldn't have to suffer rejection. What a blessing!

Mostly because of Marleen's efforts, I have the editors of the following publications to thank for including my poems in their journals and anthologies: *Atlanta Review*; *Fire and Rain*, *Eco-Poetry of California*; *Mezzo Cammin*; *California Quarterly*; *Temenos Journal*; *Light of Consciousness Magazine*; *The Mindful Word*; *Dove Tales 'Nature' Writing for Peace*; *Pilgrimage* (CSU-Pueblo); *IthicaLit*; *Marin Poetry Center Anthology*; *Pandemic Puzzle Poems*; *Abrazos & Letters from the Self to the Word*; *Birdland Journal*; and *Unsilenced, The Spirit of Women*.

Deep appreciation to my meditation teachers and students over the years for sharing their time and wisdom in classes and on retreats, with special thanks to Anna Douglas, a founding teacher of Spirit Rock Meditation Center, whose guidance and generosity of spirit welcomed me home.

I wouldn't be much of a Buddhist if I didn't acknowledge all the causes and conditions of my life that contributed to the possibility of writing this volume, including: the benign neglect form of parenting that was in style in the 1950s that left me free to roam alone in the various natural settings of my childhood; my parents' deep appreciation of creativity, their ethical principles and joie de vivre; my brothers' protection and lifelong friendship; the chronic physical pain that made me cranky but also more empathetic, and later on in life forced me to leave a stressful and unskillful livelihood, making room to rediscover meditation, its healing power, and the possibility of accessing inner wisdom; my dear childhood friend's invitation to get an apartment together, so that, though employed, I also enjoyed the unique experience that was the Haight Ashbury District of San Francisco in 1966-67, with all that entailed…both the partaking of psychedelics and the realization that the fleeting state of clarity could become sustainable if I chose the more wholesome path of meditative practice. My children's strength of character, love, and friendship has also made my life rich and given my heart ease, making room for me to pursue my passion for poetry and teaching the dharma. And, I'll end where I began, with ongoing gratitude to my husband of over half a century. You make it easy to be me.

www.ingramcontent.com/pod-product-compliance
Lightning Source LLC
Chambersburg PA
CBHW062019040426
42447CB00010B/2059